LAMBORGHINI TRACTORS

Jonathan Whitlam

AMBERLEY

Author's Note

This book is not designed to be a full technical history of the Lamborghini tractor; instead it is a broad overview of the main models produced by this Italian firm, although by no means all of them. All horsepower and similar figures are approximate and should only be used as a rough guide. All views expressed are my own, as are any errors that might have crept into the text.

As I live in the United Kingdom, the book deals with the later machines that were sold into this country in more depth than the earlier tractors, as these were the machines that I have had personal experience with.

I would like to thank Francesco Vigano from Same Deutz-Fahr for all his invaluable help and assistance and for opening the company's archives to provide the many images used in this book from the SDF Historical Archives, Treviglio, Italy.

First published 2023

Amberley Publishing
The Hill, Stroud,
Gloucestershire, GL5 4EP

www.amberley-books.com

ISBN: 978 1 3981 1333 6 (print)
ISBN: 978 1 3981 1334 3 (ebook)

British Library Cataloguing in Publication Data.
A catalogue record for this book is available from the British Library.

Typeset in 10pt on 13pt Celeste.
Typesetting by SJmagic DESIGN SERVICES, India.
Printed in the UK.

Contents

Introduction

The name Lamborghini is synonymous the world over for being carried by the sleekest, fastest and most stylish of performance sports cars. What a lot of people do not realise, though, is that the man behind the name, Ferruccio Lamborghini, not only came from an Italian farming family, but he also began his rise to engineering excellence by building the humble farm tractor.

The famous television presenter Jeremy Clarkson, who, on his latest hit show *Clarkson's Farm*, decided to purchase a huge Lamborghini R8.270 tractor to do the farm work, has highlighted this fact recently, particularly in Great Britain. Of course, with Jeremy's career being built on presenting such fast-car based television series as *Top Gear* and *The Grand Tour*, his choice is, perhaps, very predictable!

To many viewers, the existence of a Lamborghini tractor was a surprise, although others, such as myself, have actually grown up with the Italian machines. Although no Lamborghini tractors were sold in the UK until the mid-1970s, the brand did then become popular, especially in those areas of the country near a dealership.

I spent my younger years watching a large fleet of Lamborghini tractors at work during the late 1970s and through the 1980s and then on into the 1990s, the white tractors making a striking contrast among the more common Ford, Massey Ferguson and John Deere machines. They certainly made an impact on me; their distinctive styling and features made them appear a step up from the norm, especially in the late 1970s and early 1980s.

There were several farming businesses in my area that ran Lamborghini tractors thanks to the closeness of an Eastern Counties Farmers dealership that sold the brand alongside other makes and products. This resulted in the white tractors from Italy being very familiar to me, and the largest farmer who ran them was literally on my doorstep, his nearly 1,000 acres of arable and grassland being farmed originally by Nuffield tractors and then Leyland machines, before these began to give way to Lamborghini models following the purchase of a 1978 854DT. From there on, white tractors would dominate with six of them being run simultaneously at one point, and gradually updated through time to include the evolution of the Lamborghini product right up to the end of the 1990s. Seeing these tractors on an almost daily basis obviously had an effect on my interest in tractors and farming, and therefore the name Lamborghini was already, to me at least, a name synonymous with well designed and engineered tractors.

As with many famous names, this Italian brand had a long history before their introduction to the shores of my home country, dating right back to the end of the 1940s, before really taking off in Italy during the 1950s. The company was quick to realise the value of diesel engines, beginning production of its own units and during the 1960s it was also an early producer of four-wheel-drive tractors, following this up by producing the first Italian-built tractor with a full synchromesh transmission.

These innovations led to increased market share and exports around the world, and ultimately to the takeover of Lamborghini by fellow Italian tractor manufacturer SAME in 1973, under who's ownership the brand not only continued to flourish, but grew in scope and size and still remains a dedicated brand within the current SDF company.

The instigator of all this success was one man: Ferruccio Lamborghini. It is naturally with this visionary engineer that our story of the Lamborghini tractor begins.

Two very different generations of tractor working together on a Suffolk farm: a Lamborghini R854 from 1980 plants sugar beet behind a 1996 Lamborghini Formula 135 and power harrow.

The famous Lamborghini badge, familiar on the front of performance sports cars, and also proudly worn on many generations of Lamborghini tractors.

CHAPTER 1

Italian Masterpiece

Ferruccio Lamborghini was born on 28 April 1916 to a farming family in the rural Province of Ferrara in Northern Italy, and was the eldest of five sons. Despite his very agricultural upbringing it was clear, even from a young age, that he had a natural talent for working on engines and cars rather than in the fields and vineyards. Upon leaving school he began training in the workshop of a local blacksmiths, where he learnt basic iron working and welding skills. It was not long before he was then hired by the owners of the most important workshop in the whole of Bologna before finally opening his own workshop in Renazzo, in collaboration with his lifelong friend Marino Flippini. At this point Ferruccio was only eighteen years of age and his engineering aptitude was already beginning to manifest itself.

With the outbreak of the Second World War, Ferruccio found himself posted to the Isle of Rhodes with the 50th Autoreparto Misto di Manovra division of the Italian armed forces, working on the repair and maintenance of all the military vehicles on the island. However, on 8 September 1943, the military staff fled the city as Italy began to crumble as a military force. This did not deter the young Ferruccio, who soon returned to Rhodes as a civilian and opened a small workshop that he ran successfully for several years.

On his return to Italy in 1947, Ferruccio saw an opening in the farm tractor market, at that time dominated by Fiat, Landini and Motomeccania, and decided to produce an affordable but powerful tractor suited to the smaller farms that dominated his local area. To keep the sales price of his new machine as low as possible, he sourced war surplus engines and other components to produce his first tractor, the 'Carioca', which he launched in February 1948.

The tractor, designed as a low cost but reliable machine for the typical small farms of the area, was an instant success and, with the help of a loan, he purchased a thousand Morris six-cylinder engines, hired staff and began to produce his own tractors at premises in Pieve di Centro, within the metropolitan city of Bologna.

This led to Lamborghini introducing his first fully integrated tractor design using new components, which he launched as the L33 in 1951. This machine was painted a light blue, except for the wheel centres, which received a red colour. Powered by the

The 'Carioca' was the first tractor to be built by Ferruccio Lamborghini.

Using a Morris engine, Lamborghini sourced various war surplus components to assemble the 'Carioca' tractor and in the process entered the tractor building business.

Morris six-cylinder 3.5-litre petrol engine, the L33 was a reliable performer and the first Lamborghini tractor proper. Not content with just using the Morris engines as they were, Lamborghini also began fitting his own patented fuel atomiser that allowed the tractor to start on petrol before being switched to cheaper diesel fuel. This was quite an innovation at that time.

Above: The Lamborghini L33 tractor arrived in 1951 and was painted in a distinctive light blue colour. Power came from a Morris six-cylinder petrol engine fitted with a fuel atomiser to allow it to run on diesel fuel once warm.

Right: Contemporary advertising for the Lamborghini L33 of 1951.

Tractor production was now reaching 200 units a week and Ferruccio was employing thirty workers. 1951 also saw the purchase of a 10,000 square metre field and old racetrack, which then became the site of a new factory as the company 'Trattori Lamborghini' was officially born. A sales network was established and the factory continued to grow, especially after obtaining a license to build German MWM diesel engines in Italy, followed by the Italian Government's decision to grant loans to farmers for the purchase of farm machinery, which provided an extra boost in sales as farmers suddenly found cash readily available to invest in new machinery.

1952 would be a landmark year for the company, with the launch of no fewer than four new tractor models. These machines featured a new, sleeker look with a curved bonnet design painted red and contrasting with a light grey chassis and red wheel centres. These modern-looking small tractors were powered by MWM-Benz DW415 diesel engines, and were still very much aimed at the small family-run Italian farms. The DL25 model was typical of the range with its overhead valve 2.5-litre, two-cylinder engine producing 25hp at 1,500rpm, its MWM engine being equipped with a Bosch fuel injection system. Hydraulic acting rear brakes and a four-speed transmission gave the DL25 a fairly high specification for the time. The range was increased in 1953 by the addition of the more powerful DL40 and DL50 models.

The DL15 was the smallest of four brand new tractors introduced by Lamborghini in 1952 and painted in a new red colour scheme.

This rear view of the Lamborghini DL15 shows the simple drawbar arrangement and large belt pulley.

The DL20 shared the same styling as the DL15, but offered more power output from its MWM engine.

MOTORE: a ciclo Diesel MWM BENZ - 2 cil. - 4 tempi - HP 17/20 - raffreddamento a circolazione d'acqua a mezzo pompa - lubrificazione forzata a pompa - regolatore registrabile - filtro aria a bagno d'olio - Consumo medio orario di carburante Kg. 1,500.

INIEZIONE: a precamera - taratura iniettori atm. 120

IMPIANTO ELETTRICO: con batteria 12 V. a 3 fari Dinamo e motorino avviamento Bosch.

FRIZIONE: monodisco a secco.

CAMBIO: a 4 marcie e retromarcia - rapporti di velocità Km/ora 3 - 5 - 10 - 16 - retromarcia 2,20.

DIFFERENZIALE: ad ingranaggi conici con riduttore ed albero presa di forza.

FRENI: meccanici sulle ruote posteriori.

DIMENSIONI DEL TRATTORE:
Altezza massima . . . . mt. 1,25
» libera dal suolo . . . . . » 0,35
Lunghezza massima . . . . . » 2,20
Larghezza » . . . . » 1,42

PNEUMATICI "PIRELLI TRACTOR":
Posteriori 9-24
Anteriori 4,00-15

PESO DEL TRATTORE: . . . . . Kg. 1300

RIFORNIMENTI: serbatoio nafta litri 20 - olio motore Kg. 5 - olio cambio Kg. 3,500 - olio differenziale Kg. 15 - olio scatola puleggia Kg. 1,500.

PULEGGIA POSTERIORE diam. cm. 25x13 a veloc. variabile col cambio giri 200 - 400 - 700 - 1000 al m'.

È un trattore di dimensioni ridotte ma di potenza notevole. È una piccola macchina idonea alle più moderne esigenze agricole e di traino.

Brochure for the Lamborghini DL20 showing its main features.

With 25hp on offer from its 2.5-litre, two-cylinder MWM engine, the Lamborghini DL25 was a very popular choice for Italian farmers in the early 1950s

Above: The Lamborghini DL25 complete with rear-mounted rotary cultivator with basic linkage to lift the implement in and out of work.

Left: The little DL25 shared the same distinctive styling as the rest of the DL tractor range, including the streamlined-style bonnet.

Above left: Contemporary brochure for the Lamborghini DL25 highlighting the use of Lamborghini's own engine.

Above right: Brochure for the Lamborghini DL30 detailing the Perkins P3 engine fitted to this model.

Right: The DL30 range of tractors also included the use of an engine designed and built in-house by Lamborghini.

The DL40 shared the same design features as the earlier models despite being more powerful. This and the larger DL50 were launched in 1953.

TRATTORI
LAMBORGHINI
CENTO

HP 20 DIESEL   HP 30 DIESEL   HP 40 DIESEL

CON MOTORI MWM-BENZ

Il tipo DL 20 a due cilindri, ha quattro marce avanti e una retromarcia con bloccaggio. A richiesta può essere corredato di barra falciante, argano e aratro automatico gommato.

Il tipo DL 30 a due cilindri, e il tipo DL 40 a tre cilindri, hanno cinque marce avanti e una retromarcia con bloccaggio. Dotati di sollevamento idraulico. A richiesta possono essere corredati di aratro monovomere, bivomere e voltaorecchio.

GOMME
PIRELLI

Costruzione trattori agricoli
LAMBORGHINI - CENTO (FERRARA) - TEL. 84

Advertising from 1953 showcasing the DL20, DL30 and DL40 models.

In 1955, Trattori Lamborghini produced its first crawler tractor, the DL 25C. This little steel-tracked machine borrowed much from the then current wheeled tractor range and was powered by either an MWM or Lamborghini 24hp two-cylinder diesel engine, driving through a four forward and single reverse gearbox. Although only 148 examples of this particular model would be built, the machine firmly put Lamborghini tractors on the map, as well as beginning a long association with tracklayers that were, and still are, an important part of farming in Italy. The slightly more powerful DL30C followed in 1957.

The DL25C was the first Lamborghini crawler and could be specified with either MWM or Lamborghini's own 24hp two-cylinder diesel engine.

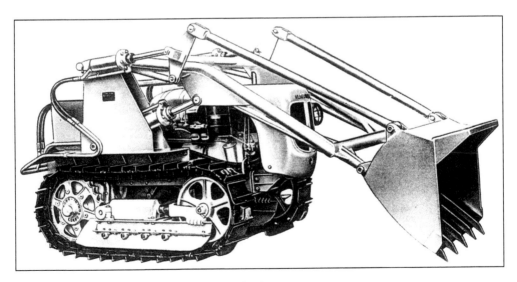

Lamborghini DL25C with heavy-duty front loader.

15

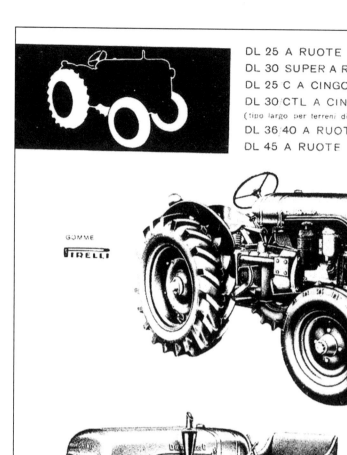

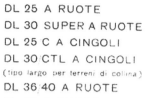

DL 25 A RUOTE
DL 30 SUPER A RUOTE
DL 25 C A CINGOLI
DL 30 CTL A CINGOLI
(tipo largo per terreni di collina)
DL 36/40 A RUOTE
DL 45 A RUOTE

GOMME
PIRELLI

machpi - bologna

LAMBORGHINI

CENTO (FERRARA)

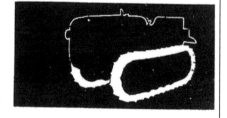

Brochure from 1956 for the Lamborghini wheeled and crawler tractor range.

16

Advertising material for the
Lamborghini DL30 CTL crawler of 1956.

1958 saw the launch of another new machine that would take the Lamborghini wheeled tractor a step further and soon became a classic. The Lamborghinietta was powered by a 2-litre, Lamborghini 22hp, two-cylinder engine, equipped with a three speed transmission and originally painted in a yellowish orange livery, perhaps to differentiate it from what had gone before, but was soon out-shopped with orange tinwork, light blue mechanicals and orange wheel centres. So successful was this design that it later spawned a whole family of similar models and was a type that remained dear to creator Ferruccio Lamborghini right to the end of his life. It was also one of the first Lamborghini tractors to be fitted with a hydraulic three-point linkage and was the Lamborghini tractor model that would usher in the 1960s.

In 1958 the Lamborghinietta appeared,
a very successful design that would
soon start its own family of models.
Power came from a 22hp two-cylinder
Lamborghini engine.

Four-wheel drive was also offered later on the Lamborghinietta, making it an even more versatile machine.

Two Lamborghinietta tractors parked together showing the orange and red eras of this model, as well as the graceful bonnet design.

Lamborghinietta tractors are still highly thought of, particularly in their native Italy, and are very sought-after by collectors and enthusiasts.

CHAPTER 2

Taking on the World

In the 1960s Trattori Lamborghini was continuing to grow, its 400 employees managing to produce around twenty-five to thirty tractors a day as the firm became a leader in the smaller agricultural tractor market in Italy. This success was fuelled by the introduction of new models, such as the 1R, a 26hp tractor powered by a two-cylinder air-cooled 1.5-litre engine that arrived in 1961. A new feature was the fitting of a three-speed transmission that had its number of gear ratios effectively doubled by the use of a high and low selector. The similar 2R model arrived in 1962, these tractors being the first Lamborghinis to offer the option of four-wheel drive on the 2R DT variant.

The first Lamborghini tractor to be offered with four-wheel drive was the 26hp 1R first seen in 1961. With a sturdy design of front axle, the four-wheel-drive 1RDT was a very capable little machine.

Above left: Front cover of the brochure for the original Lamborghini 1R.

Above right: A 1965 Lamborghini brochure featuring the four-wheel-drive version of the 1R and 2R.

This was the early 1960s and, by comparison, tractors in Britain were very different. In 1962 the Massey Ferguson 35 was very popular, as was the competitive Fordson Super Dexta that had just been introduced. Although the Massey Ferguson 35 did have the Multi-Power gear splitter as an option, neither was available with four-wheel drive. Even the larger Fordson Super Major and Massey Ferguson 65 models were only sold as two-wheel-drive tractors, making the Lamborghini 2R DT seem pretty ahead of its time. Although of course it was not offered in the UK.

1962 was also the year that Ferruccio Lamborghini first considered the idea of producing cars after having a bad experience with his Ferrari. The result was the first Lamborghini car, launched the following year. The beginning of car production did not mean that he was taking his eye off the ball when it came to tractors though; in fact the rest of the decade would see further improvements and refinements to the range.

The arrival of the new R230 marked a major change in Lamborghini tractor production in 1966. For a start it wore a new colour scheme of blue chassis and white tinwork with white wheel centres, as well as a newly designed bonnet with much squarer lines than previous efforts. This tractor, powered by a two-cylinder, 30hp, 1.5-litre diesel engine was derived from the popular 1R model with increased power and slightly larger tyres. Its big claim to fame though was the fact that it was the first Lamborghini tractor to come with a synchromesh transmission as standard, in this case a six forward and two reverse unit.

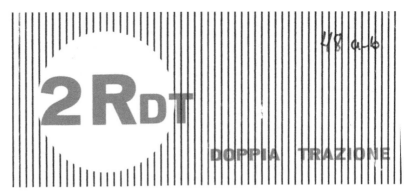

Front cover of the brochure for the Lamborghini 2R from 1966.

Just how radical this was can be judged by the fact that it took until 1981 for Ford to offer a synchromesh transmission on its tractors, for example.

The new design was carried forward over other new models including the R340, also available in four-wheel-drive format as the 340DT, and also the crawler range. In 1968, the more powerful R480 and 480 DT saw the colour scheme tweaked with the loss of the blue chassis in favour of black, making more of a contrast against the off-white of the tinwork and wheel centres. The new look tractors were in many ways a sign of the success of the Lamborghini company, and were a pointer towards the designs to come during the 1970s.

21

A new, mainly white colour scheme with blue mechanicals was chosen for the R230 tractor introduced in 1966, complete with new styling and powered by a two-cylinder, 30hp diesel engine derived from that used in the 1R. It was the first Lamborghini tractor to be equipped with a synchromesh transmission as standard.

Above left: The vineyard version of the R230 was extremely narrow and ideal for the task it was designed for.

Above right: A 1969 brochure for the R230 in its white and blue livery.

The 480DT of 1968 saw black painted mechanicals contrast with the white tinwork.

The two-wheel-drive version of the 480DT was the R480; identical except for the lack of a powered front axle.

As the 1960s entered its final years, a very large order from South America was about to cause serious issues for the business. The big order of tractors for Bolivia had been built and was awaiting shipment from the factory when a military coup in the country led to the order being cancelled at almost the last minute, resulting in the frightening total of 5,000 tractors standing unsold at the Lamborghini factory in 1970. This, and problems with strikes among the labour force caused by the trade unions in the late 1960s and early 1970s, saw Ferruccio Lamborghini begin to loose faith in his car and tractor building enterprises. The result of this change of heart by the proprietor would soon begin to show itself in the general running of the business and in the end would have very far-reaching consequences.

By the spring of 1971 the financial situation had begun to improve but the founder of the business had made up his mind and change was in the air. In 1971 some of the buildings on the factory site were sold to fellow Italian tractor and motor vehicle builder FIAT and, in 1973, Ferruccio sold Trattori Lamborghini to SAME. Ferruccio Lamborghini had been building tractors for twenty-six years, and had kept the firm that bore his name ahead of much of the competition when it came to engineering innovation and the production of a reliable product that suited the smaller farmers of the world as well as his native Italy.

And he did not stop there, as the same sort of problems in production was also affecting his automotive business. After then selling his car business to Porsche, Ferruccio Lamborghini moved to a farm in Lake Trasimeno and concentrated on a new project – that of producing Lamborghini wine. There was probably only one make of tractor that he employed on his vineyard though!

The Lamborghini brand continued in the hands of fellow Italian tractor maker SAME and, despite the founder no longer being involved, the Lamborghini name would remain a familiar sight on the side of tractor bonnets. Standing for Societa Accomandita Motori Endotermici, SAME was established in Italy in 1942 by Francesco Cassani, who had built his first diesel-powered tractor in 1927. SAME began by producing self-propelled mowers before building its first tractor proper in 1948. The DA25DT, introduced in 1952, was not only the first four-wheel-drive SAME, but also the first to be fitted with an air-cooled full diesel engine of a type that the make would soon become synonymous with. SAME claimed the DA Series were the first ever standard tractors with four-wheel drive, and the firm would remain a world leader in this technology in the future. In addition, lower link sensing rear hydraulics first appeared on the SAME 340 model of 1958. SAME tractors soon became renowned for these innovative features and the bright red colour scheme became a common sight on farms and vineyards in Italy and other countries around the world.

In 1960 the 480 was the largest tractor in the SAME range with 82hp being produced by its four-cylinder, air-cooled engine. Soon model names would be adopted for the various SAME tractors and it was the Leone and Centauro tractors that really made an impact in Britain when they began to be sold in 1964, usually in four-wheel-drive form. Their V4 engines provided 67hp and 55hp respectively. The UK was just one example of SAME's expansionist plans and during the 1960s many importers were appointed in various countries. Then Lamborghini joined the fold in 1973 and things would never be quite the same again – for either firm.

The SAME Drago and Leone were among the first SAME tractors to be imported into the UK from 1964 and their success, due to their four-wheel-drive and air-cooled engines, would see Lamborghini tractor models follow them as the 1970s progressed and the Italian brands expanded their sales worldwide, following the takeover by SAME of Trattori Lamborghini in 1973.

CHAPTER 3

The Blue Line

The two-wheel-drive R904, and its four-wheel-drive variant the R904DT, was introduced in 1972, before the SAME takeover, and would remain in production afterwards, setting the trend for a new model numbering system that reflected not only approximately the rated horsepower figure, but also the number of cylinders in the engine. As such, this was a large tractor fitted with a four-cylinder engine producing 90hp and was originally sold with blue chassis and off-white tinwork before the mechanicals were later painted black.

The front cover for a sales brochure for the Lamborghini R904 model of 1972.

Il Lamborghini
LINEA BLU
904

potenza · comfort · sicurezza

Nella nuova versione
ancora migliorato
nelle caratteristiche
nel comfort
nelle prestazioni

Above: R904DT tractors head a line-up of Lamborghini tractors in the factory yard awaiting dispatch.

Left: Front cover of a 1969 brochure for the Lamborghini 904 showing the four-wheel-drive 904DT version.

The styling of the 904 was an evolution of the earlier designs, with even more angular bonnets, and this was perpetuated by the new three-cylinder 503 and 603 tractors that followed in 1973, and were sold in either two-wheel-drive or four-wheel-drive formats. The 503 was powered by a Lamborghini 2.8-litre engine producing 47hp and driving through a 12-speed transmission. The same engine was used on the 603 with different fuelling producing 56hp.

The new angular look was perpetuated across the Lamborghini wheeled and crawler range in the early 1970s before a new model, appearing in 1975, would see a new design emerge to eventually encompass the whole Lamborghini tractor line-up. This was also the first evidence of the bringing together of the SAME and Lamborghini tractor ranges in the sense of sharing various components, most noticeably cabs. These new stylish cabs were built for the company by Italian firm SIAC, a fellow Italian business that began in 1966. The use of a common cab brought a unity to the three ranges, despite the different colours and finishing that kept the brands distinctive.

The first of this new paradigm of models was the Lamborghini 754, which, as with the earlier models, was produced in both R754 two-wheel-drive format and as the 754DT four-wheel-drive tractor. A Lamborghini 984P four-cylinder, 3.6-litre, air-cooled engine powered the first 754 tractors, although this was later swapped towards the end of production in 1982, for a larger capacity Lamborghini 105 4P 4.2-litre power plant rated at a slightly less powerful 72hp. Air cooling though would remain as a mainstay of the range along with the SAME tractors of the era.

Above: A brochure cover featuring the new 754DT model introduced in 1975, which began a new generation of Lamborghini tractors following the takeover by SAME in 1973.

Right: 1981 brochure for the Lamborghini 754, which included a line drawing of the tractor rather than a photograph.

Inside the cab of a well-used 754, showing the inside of the SIAC-built cab and the single centrally mounted gear lever.

The twelve-forward and three-reverse synchromesh transmission was controlled by a gear lever mounted centrally over the transmission tunnel, between the operators legs, as on the earlier models. The new innovation was the new SIAC quiet cab fitted from 1976, which offered much better driver comfort than the earlier cabs that were, in truth, not much more than an afterthought. Now, the cabs were designed as an integral part of the tractor design and the brand-new bonnet tinwork and flat rear mudguards helped to integrate the cab within the overall look of these new machines. The end result was a very pleasing design that looked 'right' and perhaps even more importantly, felt 'right' to the operator, the cab giving an almost flat floor area despite the central gear lever, as well as plenty of glass area for excellent all-round visibility from the driving seat. Slender cab pillars helped in this regard despite still offering built in strength to protect the operator in the event of a rollover accident. The noise levels were very quiet for their time and easily met the maximum sound level at the driver's ears in many countries, as long as the windows remained shut. Lots of sound deadening cladding was applied to the interior of the cab to lower noise levels and the end result was a very pleasant place in which to work a long day, easily equal, if not superior, to other manufacturer's offerings.

To provide ventilation in hot weather and heat in cold conditions, a fan was fitted with air outlets strategically positioned around the cab. For added air circulation the cab side windows and the front windscreen could be opened, as well as the large rear screen. The fuel tank was cleverly built into the cab design and was mounted at the rear, but low enough to make filling easy and prevent too much interference with rearwards vision.

The bonnet of the 754 featured an even squarer design than the earlier models, but one that was much cleaner than that used previously, and included a series of square cutouts along both sides – a feature that would become standard on the Lamborghini product as the 1970s drew on, and still does to this very day.

The following year, 1976, saw the introduction of the next new model in what would become known as the 'Blue Line' range thanks to the colour of its new decals on the sides of the bonnet. The new model was very similar to the original 754 but had a little more power, the new 854 being rated at 82hp from its four-cylinder air-cooled 4.2-litre engine. Once again a 12-speed synchromesh transmission was fitted and there was the choice of either the two-wheel-drive R854 or the four-wheel-drive 854DT. The 754 and 854 therefore set the pattern for the rest of the range that would be gradually introduced over the next six years.

1977 would see two new models appear at either end of the power spectrum, with the 654 being a smaller version of the 754, with a Lamborghini 984P 3.6-litre, four cylinder engine, which was of course air-cooled as was now standard on the Lamborghini and SAME ranges.

This Devon-based R754 has spent its long working life on a livestock farm and the cab has been removed to allow access to low buildings. Despite its cosmetic appearance, it is probably used every day of the year on the farm.

A newer 754DT that is also a livestock tractor complete with MX front loader. Tinwork is rusty or missing as is often the case on an older machine used exclusively on a livestock holding.

An R854 shown at work in Britain two decades after it left the factory in Italy. Equipped with dual rear wheels for sugar beet drilling, it is also fitted with a front frame for the mounting of a twelve-row hoe.

The 854 was the second model to follow the design cues of the 754 with square-cut bonnet and louvres to the bonnet covering the 82hp, 4.2-litre, four-cylinder, air-cooled Lamborghini engine. A later black radiator surround has been fitted to this machine, which was originally white.

Another view of the R854 from Suffolk, this time shown taking a break from mowing grass for silage. Launched in 1976, the 854 soon proved a popular tractor in many countries, including the UK.

The four-wheel-drive variant of the 854 was the 854DT. This is another British example and is a very late model dating from 1984. Note the tinted glass fitted to the cab windows and black painted surround to the front radiator grille, which replaced the white of the original models.

Publicity image of the 654DT, with open deck and rollover frame, taken in Italy.

Front cover of a brochure for the Lamborghini 654DT.

The other new model was much larger and was the most powerful Lamborghini tractor to date. Called the 1056, this was, as the model number suggested, a 105hp, six-cylinder machine with originally a 5.4-litre engine, later replaced by a slightly larger capacity 5.5-litre unit, still producing 105 horses. The R1056 or 1056DT, depending on whether four-wheel drive was fitted, was the first Lamborghini tractor of over 100hp and was an impressive beast, sharing the same styling as the smaller models and also the SIAC cab. The longer bonnet concealed the six cylinder power plant, making this machine look very impressive indeed.

It would be these new tractors that would be at the forefront of the Lamborghini tractors introduction to the UK market for the first time. From 1977 Maulden Engineering of Flitwick, in Bedfordshire, took on the distributorship of the white tractors, offering a range of 38 to 105hp Lamborghini tractors to British farmers. SAME tractors had been offered in the UK since the mid-1960s, but this was the first time the Lamborghini brand had been represented and it caused quite a stir in agricultural circles, resulting in sales gradually increasing during the remaining years of the 1970s as British farmers began to realise the benefits of this 'new' Italian range.

The most popular models in the UK were the 754 and 854, the 70 to 85hp sector of the market being the most popular at that time. This was a versatile size of tractor that suited both livestock and arable enterprises well, and with the choice of factory-fitted four-wheel drive, the Lamborghini models were seen as a high specification product at the time.

This R1056 has spent its entire working life on farms in Suffolk, England. The 1056 was the largest Lamborghini tractor when the brand began to be sold in the UK in 1977, and with 105hp on tap was a pretty large machine at the time. (Photo: Chris Lockwood/Anglian Agri Media)

The popularity of the 854 model in particular was emphasised to me, in particular, by the fact that the 1,000-acre farm in north-east Suffolk that I grew up next to ended running no fewer than three of these models in its tractor fleet. The first was a 1978 854DT, this being the very first Lamborghini tractor in a then fleet of Leyland machines. The Italian newcomer was very well received and its regular driver often commented on its superiority over the farm's 82hp Leyland 804 tractor, in terms of power output, traction and general comfort. It was used for many different tasks as befitted a mixed farm, from cultivation work to carting duties, manure spreading, hedge trimming and mowing. Its last role before finally being sold was as the basis for a Lely sprayer with front and rear tanks fitted.

As time moved on a second-hand R854 joined the farm, this being the very last two-wheel-drive tractor to ever be bought by the business. New in 1980, this tractor was only a couple of years old when acquired by the farm and was fitted with a simple 'A' frame front linkage to which a Lely front-mounted sprayer boom was initially fitted, the tank being carried by the rear linkage. This was short lived however, and the tractor soon settled down to a variety of other duties including mowing, carting, sugar beet hoeing, weed wiping with a Matrot implement and also powering a Moreau six-row sugar beet topper with spout for loading into side running trailers. In its later years on the farm, on which it remained for over two decades, it was mainly used for drilling sugar beet with a twelve row Matco precision planter, this being the very last task for which it was used in Suffolk before being sold, and at the time being the penultimate Lamborghini tractor left on the holding.

In 1984 a third 854 joined the farm, this time another four-wheel-drive 854DT model. This was a very late example of this type and came complete with a black surround to the radiator that made the old design fit in more with the then new models coming out of Italy. Indeed, this was the very last type of this design to arrive on this farm, making a total of six of this series to have worked in this part of Suffolk. The second 854DT was a real jack-of-all-trades and was used for a huge variety of jobs including round baling, mowing, carting, hoeing sugar beet, spreading fertiliser and manure, hedge trimming, power harrowing and other cultivations, and also drilling all the cereal crops with mainly a Roger pneumatic drill.

The new models were selling well, both at home in Italy, and also in markets such as Britain, expanding on the earlier success of the Lamborghini brand. This would only increase as more new models followed. 1978 saw the introduction of the mighty Lamborghini 1256DT, an even larger tractor powered by a 125hp, air-cooled Lamborghini 6.2-litre, six-cylinder engine, ousting the 1056 as the largest in the range, although still equipped with the 12-speed synchromesh gearbox.

The following year saw perhaps the most unusual member of the 'Blue Line' range arrive in the shape of the 955 model. With 92hp on tap from a 5.2-litre Lamborghini air-cooled engine, the power unit was a five-cylinder design, never a popular configuration with tractor engines, but one that Fiat and SAME made use of with much success. The 955 was no different and was an extremely gutsy tractor, performing well above its power rating and with plenty of torque available for heavy draft work while remaining fairly compact and relatively light in weight compared to a comparable six-cylinder machine.

Two of these unusual tractors were to join the farm near me in Suffolk. The first was a brand-new 955DT that arrived in 1982 and would go on to become the farm's main frontline machine, a second second-hand 1980 example soon joining it, the pair working many thousands of hours together over the course of the next decade and a half. I found the

The six-cylinder, air-cooled, 125hp 1256DT was an even larger tractor introduced in 1978. This open platform example is seen undergoing trials in Italy on deep ploughing work.

Another shot of the open platform 1256DT deep ploughing while a smaller Lamborghini spreads manure in the background.

Front cover of a brochure for the 1256 complete with SIAC quiet cab, the same as fitted to the smaller tractors in the range.

Front cover of another version of the 1256 brochure, making use of some ancient Italian scenery! In the end this model would have a fairly short production life as it was ultimately decided to adopt water-cooled engines in tractors of this power and larger.

four-wheel-drive 955DT to be a very impressive tractor, both these examples being extremely powerful machines that did not seem to find any task too arduous. They were certainly put through their paces during their first years in Suffolk, doing much of the ploughing work with four furrow Dowdeswell ploughs and later Krone examples, plus cultivation work with wide folding harrows and also Krone power harrows. In addition to this, the newer of the two was the regular grass chopping tractor, powering a JF FCT110 forage harvester with large silage trailers towed behind and the two would invariably form a team at this job, the other 955DT doing both the mowing and the lion's share of the carting. Another key job was pulling the farm's six-row Moreau tanker harvester when harvesting the sugar beet crop. Both tractors took turns on this job before being replaced by a self-propelled harvester in 1986. The newer

A Lamborghini 955DT pauses during sugar beet harvesting in Britain in 1985 with a Moreau six row trailed tanker harvester. Launched in 1979, this example was new in 1980.

The 955DT was an unusual tractor as its 92hp was derived from a five-cylinder, 5.2-litre, air-cooled engine. This example spent all its working life on a farm in Suffolk, England, and is shown here with a Krone power harrow. New in 1982, it clearly shows the SIAC cab in this view complete with rear opening window and rubber extensions fitted to the rear of the mudguards, as well as the rear of the fuel tank positioned under the cab.

955DT also did many years of round baling with various Krone machines; often with its sister carting the bales back to the farm with big articulated flat trailers. Carting would eventually be both tractors' main tasks, the older machine eventually being used increasingly on the dairy side of the business, spreading manure and carting bales and manure. When this tractor was sold, the newer 955DT took its place and it remained as a livestock machine right up to the 2000s when it was finally sold. It was probably these two tractors more than any others that made me realise just what special machines the Lamborghini tractors were – they just seemed unstoppable to my young and impressionable eyes!

1979 was also the year in which the SAME company was reorganized, becoming known as SAME-Lamborghini-Hurlimann, or SLH. SAME had bought the tractor business

Right: A slightly older 1980 955DT collecting round bales of straw in 1987. Access into the cab was superb on these models, using the two wide opening rearward hinged doors.

Below: Now with a new black painted front radiator surround fitted, the 1982 955DT is seen manure spreading towards the end of its life in Suffolk. The DT version was much more popular than the two-wheel-drive R variant on this model.

With good ventilation the SIAC cab was a comfortable place to spend a working day, even during the heat of summer while baling straw at harvest time. Extra work lights mounted on top of the rear mudguards allowed for work to continue after nightfall.

Hurlimann Traktoren in 1977, a Swiss firm begun by Hans Hurlimann when he built his first tractor in 1929. The resulting later models soon established the company as a producer of quality, high specification tractors with diesel power taking over from petrol in the mid-1950s, a twelve-speed transmission being introduced in 1974 and a turbocharged 155hp tractor launched as early as 1971. Sales decreased during the 1970s due to strong market competition that led to the firm taking on the Lamborghini distribution for Switzerland in 1975. This first contact, which proved very successful, eventually led to the outright purchase of Hurlimann by SAME at the end of the decade.

A new range of Hurlimann tractors, launched the same year as the forming of SLH, featured a new light green colour scheme and ranged from the H480 to the H6160, using the same SIAC cabs fitted to the Lamborghini and SAME tractor ranges of the time. Most retained Swiss-built engines, although a few featured SAME power plants and some Lamborghini and SAME models duly appeared with Swiss-built engines as their power source. Within the group, Hurlimann would remain a premium marque, with these tractors being of high specification as standard.

The use of air-cooled engines within the Lamborghini range was finally challenged in 1980 when a new, even more powerful model was introduced. This was the 1356, a tractor with a huge bonnet covering its Lamborghini six-cylinder, 135hp, 6.8-litre, water-cooled engine. The change to water-cooling was a dramatic turn and was in contrast to the large six-cylinder SAME Buffalo and Hercules tractors of comparable size, which retained air-cooling that had been adopted on the earlier 1256 model that this new model replaced.

The 1356DT was another tractor that I got to know well. A 1981 example was bought by the farm, making it its largest ever tractor. At the time, it certainly seemed massive, the

Hurlimann was originally based in Switzerland, being taken over by SAME in 1979 with the resultant reorganisation giving birth to the new SLH title for the merged enterprise. The same year saw a completely new range of Hurlimann tractors launched, all sharing the SIAC cab with the SAME and Lamborghini brands. Smallest, originally, was the H480, powered by a SAME 4.6-litre, four-cylinder engine of 82hp.

The Lamborghini 1356 was a benchmark machine when launched in 1980, not only because it was then the largest in the range, but also because it was the first to move away from air-cooled engines and embrace a water-cooled power plant when it replaced the air-cooled 1256. The Lamborghini engine was a six-cylinder, 6.8-litre block producing 135hp. This example, pictured in Britain in 1985, is equipped with dual rear wheels while breaking down ploughed land with a Krone power harrow.

SIAC cab looking almost tiny when compared to the huge white bonnet. As the largest tractor, the 1356 was used mainly for heavier cultivation work such as ploughing and cultivations, but it also managed to be used for quite a lot of carting work thanks to the farm traditionally using large ex-tipper lorries as trailers, with the cab, engine and front axle removed and a drawbar fitted in their place. These could be very heavy when fully loaded with grain or sugar beet and a tractor of the caliber of the 1356 was needed to deal with it in anything but ideal conditions.

More power was to come. The most powerful Lamborghini yet arrived in 1981 when the 1556 arrived, once again making use of a water-cooled engine with an output of a massive 155 horses. Power requirements were ever on the rise in many arable-farming areas of the world, and the manufacturers responded with ever more powerful machines. The Lamborghini 1556 certainly looked impressive enough – the same cab used from the smaller models looking rather small on this leviathan of a tractor!

As the largest Lamborghini model ever built so far, the 1556 was a long way from the roots of the company, being a huge tractor compared with the small machines that began the company back in the 1950s. There were now three big six-cylinder tractors making up the Lamborghini offering, from the 1056, through the 1356 to the range-topping 1556.

It was left to smaller models to bring the 'Blue Line' range to a conclusion, with the last models being introduced in 1982. Smallest was the 503, powered by a 2.8-litre, three-cylinder engine of 53hp, using the same twelve-speed transmission as fitted to the rest of the range, including the mighty 1556.

The 1356 was only the largest Lamborghini tractor until the following year when the impressive 155hp 1556 arrived on the scene. This publicity photograph shows the impressive lines of this beast, as well as the added extra of two work lights positioned in the cab roof line at the front.

A side view of the 1556DT also shows just how impressive this new tractor was, especially in 1981. A tall intake pipe, complete with pre-filter bowl, was placed on the front of the bonnet ahead of the exhaust stack on this model, the rest of the range featuring the air cleaner under the bonnet itself.

Front cover of the brochure for the Lamborghini 1556

Its sister tractor, the 653, was also powered by a three-cylinder engine, this time a 3.1-litre version with an output of 62hp. Both these tractors featured a smaller cab than that used on the larger models with a lower roof profile. The 684 model shared that same cab and was a four-cylinder alternative to the 653 with its 3.6-litre engine offering 67hp.

These three new models of 1982 brought the 'Blue Line' tractor range to an end. It was very much the end of an era, albeit a very successful one, these models having seen the Lamborghini brand established in ever more countries around the world as well as on its home market. In 1983, though, the first of a radical new range would appear ready to bring in a new level of style and technology to the Lamborghini tractor line.

1556

Lamborghini
TRATTORI

Puissance élevée
Refroidissement à eau
Consommation peu
élevée
Boîte synchronisée
Pont avant
autodébloquant
Adherence totale
Freins à disques à
bain d'huile

Above: The 1556 looks suitably imposing in this studio shot for another version of the brochure for this flagship machine.

Left: The German language version of the 1556 brochure featured an external shot of the Italian giant.

From the largest to the smallest – the three-cylinder, 53hp 503DTS was launched in 1982 and, along with the 653 and 684, were the last of the 'Blue Line' models to be introduced.

Export version of the Lamborghini 503DTS at work.

Vineyard version of the 503DTS was ideal for working between growing vines in the wine growing areas of Italy.

The standard version of the 503DT four-wheel-drive tractor, complete with open canopy incorporating a rollover protection frame.

Front cover of a brochure depicting the vineyard version of the 503.

CHAPTER 4

The New '6' Pack

With the 'Blue Line' tractors in full production covering a very wide range of models and sizes, and proving extremely popular in many markets, SLH was already looking to the future to see where tractor technology was going over the next decade. One of the areas of growth would be in higher horsepower models with increased driver comfort. The 1976 quiet cab legislation had spearheaded a new approach to cab comfort, with not only noise reduction, but also driver ergonomics and visibility from the seat becoming equally as important.

In 1983 the first of the new generation of Lamborghini models appeared, which would eventually form part of a completely new range of six-cylinder tractor models that were virtually new from the ground up and included a new transmission and liquid-cooled modular engines.

From the outside, the new '6 line', as they became known, looked very different from what had gone before. The off-white tinwork and black chassis remained, but a new cab with much larger glass area was now fitted with a flat floor and gear levers mounted to the right-hand side of the driver's seat. Two doors both side of the cab allowed access to the seat and these were made of single pieces of glass for maximum visibility. This was in addition to the front windscreen being fitted with full-length glass from the roofline down to the floor, either side of the bonnet, giving a huge amount of glass area compared with the earlier cab. The fuel tank was now moved to under the cab steps instead of at the rear of the cab, giving much better rearwards vision down towards the rear linkage.

The new cab was complimented by a completely new design of bonnet, with the by now distinctive square cutouts remaining, but now joined by a black radiator grille that wrapped around the front of the tractor and onto both sides, with the head lamps mounted on a narrow section beneath the front grille. Additional work lamps were included on all four corners of the cab, at both the front and rear, giving much better vision when working after dark. A new zinc coating process was applied to all the metal parts to help prevent corrosion and wide rear mudguards prevented a lot of muck and dirt spraying up onto the back of the tractor.

The baby of the new range was the 956, the model numbers still denoting the power rating and number of cylinders: this being a 95hp tractor powered by a six-cylinder Lamborghini 916.6W 5.5-litre engine, the 'W' in the engine designation standing for water-cooled – the 956 being the first Lamborghini of this size to not be air-cooled.

The smallest of the new six-cylinder range was the 95hp 956, seen here with a Claas Rolland 44 round baler working in Britain. The styling was very different on these new tractors compared to the earlier machines, and were a new concept from the wheels up, now featuring water-cooled engines.

An example of the 956 was bought new by a farm neighbouring that I grew up next to. Previously a user of Ford and Massey Ferguson tractors, this was their first Lamborghini and it was a 1987 tractor. It was mainly used for ploughing and cultivation work, as well as baling and carting duties, before spending the last years of its life in Suffolk fitted with a front-end loader.

Next up in size was the 1106, which used the same 916.6W engine as the 956 with different fuelling to up the power to 110hp. The 125hp 1306 model was the smallest to feature a turbocharged version of the same engine, now called the 916.6WT in this application, this being the essence of the modular concept adopted with this range, where a single engine design could be used with different fuelling and turbocharging to produce tractors of varying power outputs, therefore reducing manufacturing costs and spare parts inventory.

A demonstration of a very early example of the 1306, including one fitted with a front linkage and using a front and back ploughing set, the farm near me soon bought its first example of this new design of Lamborghini tractor in 1985, the new 1306 joining the 1356 as the two largest tractors on the holding. The 1306 soon proved a very versatile machine and as well as doing heavy cultivation and ploughing work, also replaced the 955 tractors on tasks such as powering the JF FCT110 forage harvester. It remained a frontline machine until 1989 when it was replaced by a new 1306, this example being equipped with a very substantial front linkage complete with power take-off. As soon as it had been delivered it was used on hire to farm machinery dealer Westmac, who used it to power both front and rear mower conditioners at a national grassland demonstration. Limited use was made of the front linkage back in Suffolk, where it was planned to be used with a front-mounted plough but it did not actually do much of this. A 6-metre-wide cultivator press was used with a 6-metre Lely power harrow on the rear making a very impressive sight, especially as the tractor was equipped with dual wheels on both front and back. A smaller press was also used on the front linkage when this 1306 was used on a Rau combination rotary cultivator and drill. Other jobs included replacing the earlier 1306 on the JF FCT110 forage harvester during its last years before round bales replaced the silage clamp. This 1306 lasted until the late 1990s before being traded in.

The 1106 was a 110hp tractor. Although two-wheel-drive versions of these models were offered, four-wheel drive was usually chosen by purchasers by this time.

An early example of the 125hp Lamborghini 1306, new in 1984 and seen with a Krone plough working in the UK in 1985.

By contrast, this is a late example of the 1306, dating from 1989, the last full year of production of the model. Apart from small detail changes, not much had changed, the most noticeable being the replacement of the tall air intake pipe on the end of the bonnet with one positioned entirely under the tinwork. Note the heavy-duty front linkage fitted along with extra work lights to replace the obscured factory-fitted items at the bottom of the radiator.

Above left: The new cab was well designed and ahead of its time in terms of ergonomics in 1983. Both cab doors opened wide on front-mounted hinges to gain access to the flat-floored cab, with the two gear levers mounted to the right of the driver's seat.

Above right: The adjustable steering column was mounted under the dashboard and gave all the basic information by means of analogue dials.

At the rear of the new six-cylinder tractors, such as the 1306, a stronger rear linkage gave more lift capacity and the lack of a rear-mounted fuel tank increased visibility when attaching to implements.

Both these 1306 tractors were impressive, but did seem to suffer more reliability issues than, for example, the previous 955DT tractors. None were too serious and both tractors were well liked on the farm, the new cabs coming in for much praise thanks to greater ease of use and comfort. Despite the new use of zinc-coated paint on the tinwork, this generation did seem more prone to corrosion than the earlier incarnations.

The next tractor in the new range, the 1506, used a Lamborghini 1106/4T 6.8-litre, water-cooled engine producing 145hp, while the new flagship model, the 165hp 1706, used a different version of the same engine dubbed the 1106/17T. These last two machines were big tractors for their day and took the Lamborghini name to new heights of power as well as style.

A 1506 did not arrive in my area of Suffolk until 1989 when a brand-new example arrived taking the top spot on the farm as it replaced a 1985 Hurlimann H-6170T that had occupied that spot for several years, this tractor itself sharing the same common platform as the Lamborghini 1706. The 1506, complete with front linkage, was chosen as it was felt there was no need for the extra power at that time, and this tractor soon began its primary cultivation role on the farm, using both front and rear Krone ploughs, 6-metre-wide power harrows and other implements. It was often used with dual wheels fitted all-round and looked very impressive when so equipped. The front and rear ploughs proved troublesome

Carting grain in Suffolk, England, with a Lamborghini 1306 and a large trailer made out of an old Leyland truck. Tinted glass in the cab and a good ventilation system aided driver comfort.

Powered by a water-cooled, six-cylinder engine and with 125 horses on tap, the 1306 could easily handle all farming tasks, including cultivations with a 6-metre-wide Bomford Dyna-Drive. Dual rear wheels helped increase traction while also reducing soil compaction.

in use, with a three furrow on the front linkage and a five furrow on the back, and although the 145hp of the 1506 could cope well enough in good conditions, much of the farm consisted of heavy clay, and when wet conditions were prevalent it proved a very difficult task for the tractor to carry on ploughing with the front set, the axle often turned almost to full lock in the furrow just to keep the whole outfit running in a straight line. Transport issues and getting the work of both front and rear ploughs to match added to the front ploughs soon being left in the nettles! The 1506 was replaced in the mid-1990s by a newer generation Lamborghini of 163hp.

Above: The 1506 was a larger model with 145hp available from a Lamborghini 6.8-litre, water-cooled, six-cylinder engine. New in 1989, this example, working a Krone five furrow plough, is equipped with a front linkage. Attached to this is a full set of wafer weights to counterbalance the heavy plough.

Right: Worm's eye view of the impressive looking Lamborghini 1506, which still looks striking after many years of hard work.

Publicity image for the most powerful Lamborghini tractor yet – the 165hp 1706.

Close-up detail of the bonnet of the 1706, including the distinctive bonnet louvres associated with the brand.

There were three transmission options available across the new '6 line' range with the basic option being a twelve-speed unit derived from that used on the previous series, or alternatively the purchaser could choose a twenty-four-speed version or a twenty-speed creeper box. The distinctive new models were also available with a factory fitted front linkage system, which allowed implements to be mounted on the front as well as the back of the tractor, a system that grew in popularity as the 1980s progressed, especially in continental Europe.

Right: Both the 1506 and 1706 kept the tall air intake pipe on top of the bonnet, including a pre-cleaner bowl, throughout their production life. The plastic cover on top of the bonnet near the cab was later omitted.

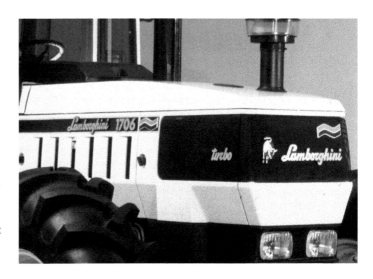

Below: A side view of the imposing Lamborghini 1706, a true powerhouse designed for the toughest tasks that 1980s farming could throw at it.

Front cover of the brochure for the Lamborghini 1706.

The same basic design was also produced in red as the SAME Laser range but with air-cooled SAME engines, as well as in Hurlimann colours as part of this Swiss range, production of which had moved from Switzerland to the SAME factory in Treviligo, now the centre of all tractor manufacturing for the group.

This range was the first to be wholly developed by the new SLH company and the development costs could effectively be spread across the three different makes; the use of major components could then be shared between the different brands while also maintaining the individuality of each brand with detail differences. This was a fairly new concept at the time, but one that has been widely copied by other tractor manufacturers since, especially after mergers and takeovers where a common platform is used for several different brands.

The Lamborghini brand might well have lost its independence, but its first decade in the ownership of SAME had seen it grow continually. The formation of SLH, and the resulting new models and shared technology, only continued to increase the success of the white tractors.

The distributorship of the Lamborghini tractors in the UK changed during the 1980s from Maulden Engineering to Universal Tractors of Brough in Yorkshire in 1983, which quickly rebranded itself as Linx Agriculture, but only survived until 1986 when SLH took things in-house and moved the operation to Barby, in Warwickshire. All three brands would now be represented by SLH themselves in Britain, supplying an ever-growing number of dealerships around the country, many of whom sold more than one of the brands.

The rear end of the 1506 and 1706 was strengthened to cope with the extra load, although the whole new six-cylinder range shared the same basic design. A glass panel at the bottom of the cab allowed for excellent vision from the seat down to the lower links.

Front view of the 1706 with marker sticks positioned to provide scale for axle width and ground clearance. The design of the 6 series models was very distinctive, especially from this angle with its bonnet lines sloping towards the bottom and tapering cab.

As the flagship model of the entire Lamborghini tractor range, the 1706 was an impressive machine and the same basic design also formed the basis for the SAME Laser 170 and the Hurlimann H-6170T, which were also the flagship models in their respective ranges.

Early publicity material for the entire new six-cylinder range, complete with the Lamborghini 'raging bull' logo.

CHAPTER 5

Racetrack Models

The styling of the '6 line' was tweaked to fit a range of four-cylinder machines in 1989, using a modified version of the cab first seen in 1983. For the first time these new tractors also had a name as well as a model number; the range was called 'Grand Prix' as a way of cashing in on the Lamborghini name and its association with motor racing and fast cars. Perhaps rather incongruous when it comes to farm tractors!

The Grand Prix range
of 1989 included
the same cab as the
six-cylinder line.
The largest was the
90hp 874-90. (James
Rosewell)

The Grand Prix range was made up of the 70hp 674-70, 80hp 774-80 and 90hp 874-90 with the old numbering system being changed, although the power was still featured, if not the number of cylinders. A twenty-speed forward and reverse transmission was fitted giving plenty of choice of ratios, but it was the 'drive by wire' engines themselves that were a sign of things to come.

Publicity photograph of an 874-90 taken in Italy complete with front linkage. The styling of these Grand Prix tractors closely followed that of the larger six-cylinder machines, such as the 956, and used the same cab.

This side view clearly shows the family resemblance to the larger six-cylinder tractors, as well as the new decals declaring the Grand Prix name and the Powerspeed transmission.

Several export markets still required an open platform and this 874-90 has been outfitted as such along with an extended air intake pipe to enable working in very dusty conditions.

Electronics had been a growing presence in the world of agricultural tractors for some time, with many manufacturers adopting electronic performance monitors and electronically controlled hydraulic systems. The Grand Prix four-cylinder engines were the first example of electronics being used in the Lamborghini range, with an electronically governed injection pump being fitted for each cylinder of the 4-litre engines to provide efficient fuelling for any task. The engines used were actually SAME power plants of the same type used in the new Explorer tractors with similar power outputs.

The use of the name Grand Prix for this range was only the beginning of a trend of using names for the various new Lamborghini ranges. Following quickly on the heels of the Grand Prix machines, the Formula six-cylinder models followed in 1990. Now complete with full electronic engine monitoring, the Formula 115 and 135 also showed off a brand-new look with a chunkier bonnet and a tweaked cab, using the same basic structure as before, but with improvements to make it even more user friendly. The SAME Antares and Hurlimann Elite ranges shared the same platform as the Formula models including the thirty-six-forward and thirty-six-reverse speed transmission.

The Formula 115 used a SAME 1000.6W 6-litre engine to produce 115hp while the larger 135 used the 1000.6WT version of the same water-cooled engine to produce 132hp, thanks to the addition of a turbocharger.

Above left: A still working Grand Prix takes a break in the picturesque and mountainous Italian scenery.

Above right: German publicity for the Grand Prix 874-90 showing the factory-fitted front linkage option.

A very work weary example of an 874-90 seen in 2021 while still a livestock machine. Despite SLH adopting zinc coating to the paintwork, the dreaded 'tin-worm' still manages to get in and cause corrosion.

In 1990 the Formula two model range appeared, and in this picture two very different generations of Lamborghini tractor are seen side by side as a new Formula 115 meets the 955DT it displaced from mainline tasks on a Suffolk farm.

The 115hp, six-cylinder Lamborghini Formula featured brand-new styling, especially in the area of the bonnet. The cab, although with new details changes, used the same frame as used on the earlier models.

Above left: The Formula 135 and 115 were the first to be fitted with a new generation of cab based on the earlier unit, but considerably updated, including a new roof molding and slightly altered front section, although still tapering towards the bonnet.

Above right: Inside the cab of the 115, the main controls are all positioned up on a console to the right of the driving seat, including the gears to operate the fifty-four-speed transmission, which was standard, or the optional creeper version, which increased the number of ratios to an incredible seventy-two speeds.

The dashboard on the Formula 115 and 135 was hugely updated on that used previously and included a graphic display of the tractor with lights to show activations of various functions.

There was also a smaller Formula 105 model based more closely on the larger Grand Prix machines and powered by a SAME four-cylinder, turbocharged, 103hp, 4-litre engine driving through a forty-speed transmission.

The first experience I had of the new Formula range was in 1990 when a demonstrator Formula 105 arrived for a few days on the farm near me in Suffolk, although it did not find favour at that time and no orders were forthcoming. The neighbouring farm, with the 956, did buy an example of this tractor, its 105 being used for drilling with a Massey Ferguson 30 for many years alongside the 956 before being replaced after about a decade by a Massey Ferguson tractor.

Although the 105 had not impressed, a larger Formula 115 was added to the tractor fleet on the farm near me in 1991. This effectively replaced the newer of the two 955DT tractors and was soon being used on a Krone plough, mowing grass for silage and doing a great deal of mainline carting duties of grass, cereals and sugar beet.

It would take until 1995 before another Formula model joined this farm in the shape of a larger 135 model, which was often used for cultivation duties with dual wheel fitted to both the front and rear. It was the very last Lamborghini tractor left on the farm and spent its final years powering a hedge trimmer.

The addition of electronic engine control was further enhanced with the launch of the Lamborghini Racing range in 1991, the first model to appear being the Racing 165. By this stage, SLH had embraced electronics and this tractor was one of the most sophisticated of any so far seen, with not only electronic engine management and electronic controls in general, but also a new twenty-seven-speed electronically operated, full powershift transmission. With power coming from a six-cylinder, 6-litre engine producing 163hp, this was a fitting new flagship model and shared much with the Formula range, especially in styling and overall external design, although a new colour scheme was adopted to give it a look somewhat apart from the other models, as perhaps befitted a tractor with such advanced electronic features.

Introduced as a baby member of the Formula range, but actually sharing much more with the Grand Prix line-up, the Formula 105 was a 103hp, four-cylinder tractor. This one is planting a cereal crop in Suffolk with a Massey Ferguson 30 drill in the early 1990s.

SLH sold the electronic powershift they had developed to other manufacturers for them to use in their own larger tractors, and it appeared in the Renault 160-94 and 180-94 models as well as the largest Deutz-Fahr machines.

Later in 1991, the Racing 165 was joined by the larger 190 model, using the same engine to produce 189hp via the use of a turbocharger. A further smaller Racing model, the 150, arrived in 1994.

With dual wheels fitted all-round, this 132hp Lamborghini 135 is preparing a seedbed for sugar beet with a power harrow in eastern England.

The Racing 165 was the first of a new generation of high horsepower Lamborghini tractors that also included the first widescale use of electronic features. The styling took its cues from the Formula 115 and 135 with new blue decals and black bonnet panels making it stand out from the earlier models.

This British example of the Racing 165 has been equipped with extra work lights on both front mudguards. A new design of large weight is carried on the front linkage and replaced the earlier wafer-style examples.

The full powershift transmission in the Racing models provided twenty-seven speeds and was controlled by this single multi-function lever beside the seat.

The Racing dashboard followed the same layout as the Formula models.

Top of the range, and now gaining the title of the largest Lamborghini tractor so far built, the Racing 190 was a 189hp giant that joined the 165 later in 1991.

A smaller Racing 150 arrived in 1994 to complete the range. Here a 150 waits beside the bigger 190 at an auction in the UK.

In 1994 the first Lamborghini Racing tractor arrived on the farm near me in Suffolk. This was a Racing 165 that replaced the existing 1506 as the largest tractor on the farm and was the first machine to feature such a level of electronic sophistication on this farm. It was soon pressed into work, along with a new seven furrow Gregoire-Besson plough that matched its power very well and from now on this tractor was responsible for all the ploughing on the holding. It was also used for cultivation work, with the now customary dual wheels fitted all round and was also used on a 6-metre-wide Lely power harrow. The Racing 165, despite its technical sophistication, performed extremely well and was a very reliable and gutsy tractor.

It was joined in 1998 by another brand-new Racing model, this time the flagship 190. This was the largest tractor ever seen on this farm before and was soon pressed into work with a 6-metre Maschio power harrow and Accord pneumatic drill combination with front-mounted hopper mounted on its factory-fitted front linkage, which also included a power take-off. Occasionally it would also do a little ploughing, but this was usually left to the 165. Unfortunately, although the 165 had given a very good account of itself during its time in Suffolk, the same could not be said of the 190. Despite looking superb and being a very powerful machine with excellent traction and comfortable cab, the 190 was plagued with reliability issues, mostly electric in nature. This often required the tractor to be towed to the local dealership as it could not be driven. After many such instances this tractor was probably the main reason why no new Lamborghini tractors were ever added to the fleet on this farm, ending a relationship that stretched back to the late 1970s.

The problems with the 190 came to an end when it was burnt out while at work in a field, a hydraulic leak spurting hot oil all over the cab, which then ignited and wrote off the machine. As for the 165, that kept on working well until finally replaced by a Caterpillar Challenger 45 of much greater horsepower.

With dual wheels fitted all-round the 163hp Racing 165 makes an impressive sight working in stubble with a set of disc harrows.

Racing 165 and 190 working together on the same farm in Suffolk. A large Accord seed hopper is fitted to the 190's front linkage.

The complete drilling rig is shown here as the Lamborghini Racing 190 plants cereals with a 6-metre-wide Maschio power harrow and Accord drill combination.

Once again, the fitting of dual wheels all-round turns the Racing tractor into an impressive looking beast. This 190 is working a 6-metre-wide Bomford Dyna-Drive at high speed.

This contrast of good and bad tractors is not something that is confined to the Lamborghini brand, and is typical of all machines as well as tractors – sometimes one just refuses to work properly. It certainly was not the norm for the Racing 190; I found one recently still working in Devon, putting many hours of work in on ploughing and cultivation work each year without any faults at all!

The Racing range may have been the largest tractors in the Lamborghini line-up built by SLH, but it was actually beaten in size by a couple of imported models introduced in 1993. SLH had begun to supply American firm Allis-Gleaner Corporation, or AGCO as it is better known, with 70 to 115hp Lamborghini models to sell in North America, badged under the White name. White was one of several companies under the control of AGCO at this time, and soon it would also acquire Massey Ferguson, followed by Fendt and Valtra. This marketing arrangement saw a reciprocating deal where the two largest White 244hp and 263hp tractors were imported in Lamborghini colours and badged as the Traction 240 and 265 models, as well as also in SAME colours. The Lamborghini-branded tractors wore a modified livery first used on the Racing tractors, which softened the angular lines of these big monster machines. They also featured an exhaust stack mounted to the side of the cab, rather than on top of the bonnet, a feature that made for excellent forwards visibility. Power came from a turbocharged six-cylinder, 8.3-litre Cummins engine driving through an eighteen-forward by nine-reverse powershift transmission. The two models were only sold for a period of four years and were the first Lamborghini-badged tractors to break the 200hp barrier. Sales were pretty limited and it does not appear that any of these tractors made their way to the UK, for example.

The Racing 190 is still an impressive machine today, and this working example is shown ploughing in Devon, England, in 2021.

A rear view of the Racing 190 shows how big this tractor actually is when compared to the driver in the seat! The Racing range was instrumental in taking the Lamborghini name forwards into the electronic age of farming.

Right: The distinctive bonnet of the Racing 190, the 'zinc' decal denoting the rust preventative treatment given to the sheet metal work on Lamborghini tractors since the early 1980s.

Below: With plenty of power to spare the 190 could easily cope with a much larger implement than this four furrow plough, even on the steep slopes of the Devon countryside.

A side view of the Racing 190 bonnet shows the distinctive Lamborghini styling and branding, which despite the large size of the bonnet is also tapered downwards towards the front to improve visibility from the cab.

Electronics feature heavily in the Racing 190 and have proven to be very robust, still working well in older and well-worked machines such as this.

The rear linkage of the Racing 190 was capable of lifting 8,601 kg, a very good figure for the time.

TRACTION 240

THE POWER MASTER

- Cummins turbo after cooled engine.

- Full Power Shift 18x9.

- "Wrap round" vision.

Lamborghini

There's no stronger bull on earth.

Front cover of a brochure for the Traction 240, the smaller of two North American-built tractors that took the power range of the Lamborghini tractor to new heights in 1993. As well as a SAME version, these tractors were also sold in Massey Ferguson colours after AGCO acquired MF in 1994.

At the other end of the spectrum, the little Runner series of smaller tractors appeared in 1993, while 1994 also saw the introduction of an updated range in the 85 to 105hp sector. The new Premium tractors replaced the larger Grand Prix versions and looked very different thanks to new curved bonnets that sloped to provide better forward visibility. Smallest of this four-model range was the Premium 850 powered by a SAME 1000.4 WT3 four-cylinder, 4-litre engine of 85hp driving through either a twenty-speed or, incredibly, a sixty-speed gearbox.

The same engine was used to power the 95hp 950 model, while a similar unit powered the more powerful 103hp 1050. A six cylinder, 6-litre version of the SAME engine was used to power the flagship 105hp 1060 model that was the largest of the range. New Grand Prix models followed using the same sloping bonnet styling as the Premium range.

The 263hp Traction 265 had no SLH involvement in its design, being originally a White tractor model based on earlier Deutz-Allis designs, including the distinctive cab. These tractors featured a cab-mounted exhaust stack, leaving the bonnet clear, and were powered by Cummins 8.3-litre engines.

A Premium 950 seen on display at the Suffolk Show when brand new. The 95hp 950 was the middle model in a range of three four-cylinder tractors launched in 1994, which included a quite prominently sloping bonnet design.

A Lamborghini Premium 850 next to a SAME Silver 90 at the Grassland '96 event in Warwickshire in 1996. The Silver range was the red equivalent to the white Premium line-up.

With 103hp available, the Premium 1050 was the largest four-cylinder model in the Lamborghini range. This British example is seen turning over its reversible plough before making another bout up the field.

Launched at the same time as the rest of the Premium range, the 1060 was the only one with a six-cylinder engine. This example shows the later option of an exhaust stack mounted beside the cab pillar rather than on top of the bonnet. It is seen at work in its native Italy.

Underneath the curved bonnet of the Premium 1060 resided a six-cylinder SAME engine of 105hp.

With the same styling as the larger Formula models, the Premium range brought the 85 to 105hp Lamborghini offering into line with the rest of the brand's line-up.

A Premium collecting grass for silage with a self-loading forage wagon in Italy.

A demonstrator Premium 1060 was briefly used on the farm near me in Suffolk but did not find favour after the Racing 190 debacle and John Deere gained the order in the end.

1993 was also, sadly, the year that marked the death of the founder of the company, when Ferruccio Lamborghini passed away aged seventy-seven. His coffin was, very fittingly, towed to his final resting place by one of his beloved Lamborghinietta tractors, this type having remained a firm favourite of his, despite all the many machines built after it. The man may have left this mortal coil, but the machines that still proudly bore his name would have much to face in an ever-changing world.

And things were indeed to change dramatically after 1995, the year that SAME bought the German Deutz-Fahr agricultural division from owners KHD. There had been a great deal of co-operation between the two manufacturers previously, with SLH not only supplying its electronic powershift transmission to KHD, it also actually assembled the largest Deutz-Fahr tractors that used it at its factory in Italy. The acquisition of the green tractor marque saw an end to the SLH company and, in due course, it was re-established as SAME-Deutz-Fahr, or SDF for short. This move would have a great impact on future Lamborghini tractor production.

Front cover of a brochure for the entire Premium range.

CHAPTER 6

The German Connection

Deutz-Fahr was the result of a merger. The first Deutz tractor appeared in Germany in 1907, with the first diesel tractor arriving in 1927. In 1938 the Klockner-Humboldt-Deutz company was formed and diesel-powered Deutz tractors were a major part of the new business. Air-cooled Deutz tractors were sold in Britain as early as 1961 and, in 1968, KHD took a major share in the fellow German Fahr business that produced tractors and farm machinery, including combines. It took until 1981 before the Deutz-Fahr brand name was adopted, by which time the very popular DX Series of Deutz-Fahr tractors, with distinctive angular styling and cab design, was selling well.

When SAME-Deutz-Fahr was formed in 1995, a new range of tractors was on the drawing board in Germany that, in due course, was launched from 1996. This range was called Agrotron and included steeply sloping bonnets and a brand-new spacious cab with plenty of glass area, making it look extremely futuristic. By the following year the Agrotron line-up extended to some ten models, ranging from 75hp to 150hp.

The German Deutz-Fahr tractors of the 1980s looked very distinctive, this Commander being a very good example of the angular styling and features first seen the decade previously.

1998 saw SAME-Deutz-Fahr launch two big green tractors, the Agrotron 230 and 260, based on the smaller Agrotron tractors scaled up to take bigger engines, which were now water-cooled, marking a big change in Deutz engine technology, moving away from the air-cooled engines that Deutz had always favoured. SAME had been moving in the liquid-cooled direction because of several factors, the most important being that governments around the world were beginning to bring in exhaust emission regulations and, unfortunately, air-cooled engines could not be made to meet these, whereas liquid-cooled power plants could.

As an aside, a Deutz-Fahr Agrotron 260 did become a regular feature of the farm near me, effectively being the replacement for the Racing 190 that burnt out. This was a very impressive machine that was never under stress on any job that was thrown at it, although its potential was perhaps never fully realised due to the Caterpillar Challenger 45 doing the heaviest work. Sadly, this tractor was the last connection that this farm retained with SDF, at least up to the present time.

1998 saw the first real indications of the impact the Deutz-Fahr acquisition would have on the Lamborghini tractor range when three new models from 120 to 150hp that,

An early six-cylinder Deutz-Fahr Agrotron at the British Grassland '96 event in 1996, one of the Agrotron's first public outings. The sharply sloping bonnet and futuristic looking 'bubble' cab would become enduring Agrotron features.

In 1998 the big Agrotron 230 and 260 tractors were launched by the new SDF company. Keeping the main Agrotron features but packing up to 260hp, these were extremely impressive machines.

in keeping with earlier model series names was called Champion, were launched. These tractors were clearly based on the Deutz-Fahr Agrotron tractors with the same cab and sloping bonnet line. They were not green though, and in fact were not white either, as a new silver and black livery was adopted for the Lamborghini range around this time.

An SDF branded 6-litre, six-cylinder turbocharged engine was used for these tractors fuelled to produce 120hp, 135hp or 150hp depending on the model. Transmissions included the choice of either an eighteen-speed powershift or twenty-seven-speed creeper gearbox. Larger Champion models arrived in 2000 based on the bigger Deutz-Fahr Agrotrons with 160, 180 and 195hp 6-litre, six-cylinder SDF engines.

The big Agrotron models also appeared in Lamborghini guise as the Victory 230 and 260 in 1999. With power ratings of 230 and 260hp respectively, and a forty-speed gearbox. Both were uprated to Victory Plus models in 2001. Although not quite as powerful as the

A SAME Rubin 150 in the foreground shows its common ancestry with the Lamborghini Champion in the background. The Deutz-Fahr Agrotron influence is clear to see.

Lamborghini Champion 135, the middle model in the Champion range, showing clearly the Agroton cab with its large glass area.

Above left: Technology was really moving on by the time the Champion arrived and many of the controls were now positioned on the armrest of the driving seat itself. A multi-function joystick controlled most functions, including the powershift transmission.

Above right: A more modern dashboard was fitted to the Champion models and owed much to automotive practice rather than what had been fitted to the earlier Racing models.

Distinctive silver paint suited the lines of the Lamborghini Champion well and represented a move away from the white colour first adopted back in 1966.

Traction 265, the Victory 260 was just as capable and unlike the earlier tractors, these were European prime movers rather than badge-engineered North American products. They may have shared a common platform with the Deutz-Fahr Agrotrons, but these were much closer to 'proper' Lamborghini tractors than the imported Traction models had ever been.

Above left: The imposing front cover of a brochure for a brand-new range of Lamborghini high-horsepower tractors – the Victory 230 and 260.

Above right: The front cover of a sales brochure for the Victory 230 and 260 models based on the Deutz-Fahr Agrotron 230 and 260.

Left: A Victory 260 ploughing at a working demonstration in Italy.

Right: Although not technically a Lamborghini from the ground up, the bonnets of the Victory models still held allegiance to earlier Lamborghini designs.

Below: A Lamborghini Victory at work with a set of disc harrows and showing the distinctive frontal treatment of these very powerful tractors.

The silver livery may not have had much in common with earlier Lamborghini colours of the past, but it did suit the lines of the tractors well and certainly made them stand out from other machines, with the Premium and Formula lines all receiving the new colour scheme. Two new Premium tractors also arrived in 2000, building on the existing range and bringing more power, with the 1100 having a 110hp, six-cylinder, 6-litre engine at its heart, while the larger 1300 used the same engine to produce 132hp, both using a twenty-four-speed transmission, with the option list even including a transmission with up to seventy-two ratios.

As the twenty-first century arrived even more Agrotron-based tractors would dominate the Lamborghini range, especially from 2004 with the introduction of the R Series models, which would eventually encompass most of the range within the R6, R7 and R8 series of tractors, all painted in dramatic silver livery.

2007 saw new styling brought to the smaller tractors in the range with the RF Series and, in 2010, the CF Series saw a return to the production of Lamborghini crawlers once again, after an absence from this area of the market.

A big new development was the launch of the Nitro Series in 2013 that was innovative enough to win awards for design the following year and featured new styling and a taller cab. The integration of Deutz-Fahr technology within the brands, which also still included

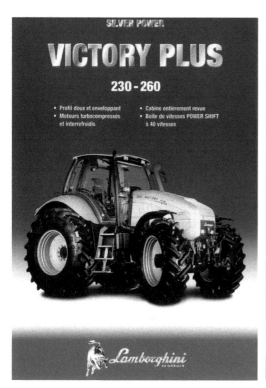

Above left: Front cover of a French brochure for the later improved Victory Plus models.

Above right: This brochure cover gives a glimpse into the superb cab of the Victory models with its armrest-mounted controls.

The silver colour scheme was also applied to the rest of the Lamborghini range, including the Formula 135. Hurlimann tractors also reverted to a sliver colour, making them look very similar to Lamborghini models around this time.

Above left: The Premium range also soon adopted the silver livery, as shown on the front cover of a brochure produced for the 850 to 1060 models.

Above right: The original Premium models looked very smart painted silver and looked much newer than they actually were. This 1060 graces the front of a brochure for the range and shows the bonnet-mounted exhaust stack instead of the by now more popular cab-mounted option.

The Premium 1300 was launched in 2000 along with the smaller 1100 model. Although featuring a new sloping bonnet, these were basically the old Formula models with a new skin.

Above left: Taking the Premium range upwards to meet the new Champion line-up was a logical step. The 1300 featured the older Lamborghini cab, but a cab-mounted exhaust stack was now a standard feature.

Above right: Premium 1300 at work with a set of rolls in Norfolk, England. With 132hp from its six-cylinder motor, the 1300 was a powerful tractor in a relatively light package.

The Grand Prix range received a significant redesign and adopted many Premium features as well as the silver colour scheme. A new, taller cab roof was also added.

SAME and Hurlimann, and the common platform design, allowed for even more sharing of components across the various brands within the group, the most obvious being the Deutz-Fahr influence with the cabs, as well as also seeing the introduction of constantly variable transmissions and electronically controlled powershift gearboxes. The future had most certainly arrived!

The R Series gradually replaced the entire Lamborghini range from 2004. This R4.105 is owned by Clive James and is equipped with an MX loader while working a Claas big baler. (James Rosewell)

With a four-cylinder engine producing 105hp, the R4.105 was part of the replacement for the Premium range. (James Rosewell)

A Lamborghini R8.265 at work in Italy with a set of disc harrows epitomizes the design and power of the largest R Series tractors of the early 2000s.

Above: The Nitro 130 VRT saw a return to a white and black colour scheme for the Lamborghini tractor. Styled by Giugiaro Design, underneath the tinwork lurked a four-cylinder Deutz engine of 127hp paired with a new continuously variable transmission giving a top speed of up to 50 kph.

Below: Futuristic interior of the cab on the Nitro 130 VRT, a clean and friendly workspace that also benefitted from the option of full cab suspension to reduce vibration.

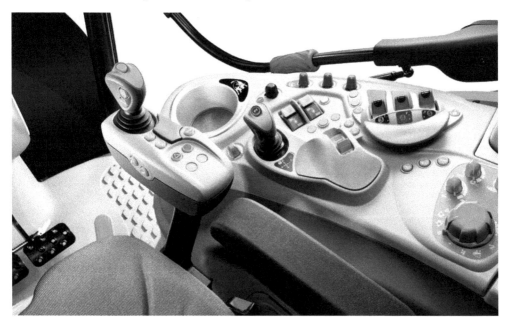

CHAPTER 7

Modern Machines

This brings us to today and, although in many countries including the UK, the Deutz-Fahr brand is now dominant, Lamborghini tractors are still produced with a full range of models and many advanced features.

The Nitro tractors gave rise to the Lamborghini tractors produced today, the Spark VRT 185 being a prime example, first introduced in 2017. Deutz engines are now the standard power units on the larger tractors, this model featuring a 188hp, six-cylinder power plant mated to a constantly variable transmission. Still using the Agrotron cab first seen in 1996, it has been considerably updated and modernised, both externally and internally.

The new cab is called the MaxiVision2 and this rear view shows clearly the extensive use of glass to provide a good all-round view for the operator. An abundance of lights, external controls and a heavy-duty rear linkage complete the package at this end of the machine.

White and black has once again made a return, replacing the recent years of silver paintwork with twenty-one models of Lamborghini produced across five ranges. This includes the Strike C, CM and CF crawlers, the Sprint and Strike small tractors that also include VRT versions with a constantly variable transmission. Spire and larger Strike models occupy the mid-range sector, while the Spark and Spark VRT models represent larger machines, with the range being topped off by the massive Mach VRT range.

To give an idea of how the modern Lamborghini tractor bristles with the very latest technology, let's take a closer look at the biggest of the lot: the Mach VRT 250. Power for this big tractor comes from a Deutz 6.1 engine using exhaust after treatment and a passive diesel particulate filter to lower emissions, while an electronic viscostatic cooling fan maximizes engine efficiency. The transmission is sourced from ZF and has four mechanical ratios within its constantly variable design that allows for a top speed of 60 kph. The

Powered by an SDF FARMotion four-cylinder engine with a maximum output of 126hp, the Spark 130 VRT sits in the middle of the three four-cylinder models that make up the Spark range.

The cab of the Spark 130 VRT is a very well appointed space in which to spend a working day, with excellent all-round vision, uncluttered layout and comfortable seat.

Above: Smaller Lamborghini tractor models today include the Spire range, which, despite their more diminutive stature, still include many of the innovative features of their larger sisters.

Below: With a 106hp available from its four-cylinder SDF FARMotion engine and the option of up to sixty gears from its powershift transmission, this Lamborghini Strike 110 is seen in the company of a more powerful SAME stablemate.

From the front, the Strike 110's styling is very imposing for what is now classed as a fairly small tractor.

computers controlling the engine and transmission continually communicate with each other automatically to maximize fuel efficiency, whatever task the tractor is engaged in. The hydraulic system is very advanced allowing for a 120-litres-per-minute flow rate with the option of a 160-litres-per-minute version. A maximum lift capacity on the rear linkage of 10,000 kg, is balanced by a front linkage with 5,480 kg maximum lift capacity, and the power take-off comes with a choice of three speed modes.

The latest generation of cab, dubbed the MaxiVision 2, is separately mounted to the engine hood to offer a quieter and more comfortable environment for the operator. An InfoCentre display, in full colour, is joined by a multifunction joystick mounted on the seat armrest to give full, electronically engaged control of the whole machine and relay information back to the driver, while SDF also offer full guidance systems that allow the tractor to drive itself in the field, controlled using GPS.

The Mach VRT 250 has 246hp available at maximum power from its 6-litre engine, concealed under a distinctively styled white bonnet, which makes it very different from those first Lamborghini tractors of 1951. It is, however, the epitome of the latest high horsepower agricultural tractor, and Ferruccio Lamborghini would perhaps be pleased that as well as these supersize tractors, his Lamborghini brand also offers so many smaller tractors still aimed at those small size farms he was once so familiar with as he grew up in his rural area of Italy, and which inspired his very first tractor.

The striking bonnet lines of the biggest current Lamborghini, the Mach 250 VRT.

Powered by a Deutz six-cylinder, 6.1-litre engine producing 246hp, the Lamborghini Mach 260 VRT is a fine successor to the large Lamborghini tractors of the past, such as the 1556, 1706 and Racing 190.

Welcome to the office! The cab of the Mach 250 VRT is as luxurious as it is practical and bristles with the latest technology, including the ability for auto guidance. With the latest constantly variable transmission, this giant Lamborghini is perhaps the easiest to drive of all and has the ability to make farming more efficient than ever before.

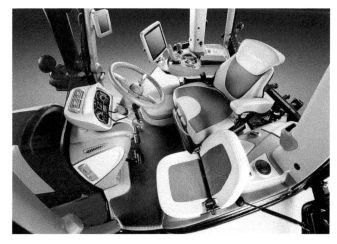

CHAPTER 8

Lamborghini Legacy

With so much innovation during its seven decades of existence, the tractors that have carried the Lamborghini name have been at the forefront of such technologies as diesel engines, four-wheel-drive systems, synchromesh gearboxes, electronic engine management, full powershift transmissions and pure and simple design flair.

Personally, as a child growing up watching a large fleet of Lamborghini tractors during the 1980s, I certainly appreciated the brand's styling and features that were, in many ways, so different from the other manufacturers offerings at the time. I was certainly impressed by the power and ruggedness of the likes of the 854DT and 955DT, as well as their excellent four-wheel drive, while the biggest tractor on the local farm, the mighty 1356DT, seemed a real giant to me back then.

As the 1980s progressed, the first 1306 arrived in the area, along with a 956 on a neighbouring farm, both of which introduced radical new styling concepts. These, and a much later 1306 and more powerful 1506, made a big impression on me too. By the time the Formula and Racing models arrived on the farm in Suffolk, I had a much wider appreciation of tractors in general, although I still found these Lamborghini models particularly impressive.

Taken in the spring of 1985, this picture shows just two of the 'Blue Line' Lamborghini tractors, out of a total of five, being used to harvest rye grass for silage and then plough it in ready for the next crop of sugar beet. One of the farm's two 955DT tractors is seen on the trailer while the farm's flagship 1356DT is on the Krone plough.

The autumn of 1985 sees a Lamborghini 955DT with a Moreau six row sugar beet harvester passing an 854DT and trailer. This 1978 854DT was the very first Lamborghini tractor on this particular farm.

As the 1990s neared their end so did the reign of the Lamborghini in my area of the country, with many local farmers already swapping to other makes and models and, finally, the big farm that had mainly inspired me succumbed to the perhaps more mediocre fair of Case IH and John Deere tractors. Therefore, to me, the 'Blue Line' and the '6 Series' in particular, are to me truly classic Lamborghini tractors and are without doubt responsible for my lifelong interest in farm tractors.

The Lamborghini name stands for speed, power, and quality in the car market to this day, and in the tractor world that same name stands for all that is the very best to be found in the form of an agricultural tractor; the type of vehicle that Ferruccio Lamborghini

This is the second Lamborghini 1306 on the farm, replacing an earlier example in 1989. It is seen sowing wheat straight after ploughing with a front-mounted press and a Ferrag Rau combination drill.

The last Lamborghini to arrive on the Suffolk farm near me was this 1998 Lamborghini Racing 190. Sadly its life was cut short after a disastrous fire, which wrote the tractor off when still only a few years old.

should perhaps be even better remembered for, his dedication to improving engines and other technology driving forward the mechanisation of farming in the twentieth century.

Lamborghini tractors still bare his name to this day – a true testimony to a visionary engineer whose roots were firmly embedded in the farming community and who never lost sight of that heritage. His tractors remain today as a lasting legacy to his forward-thinking and engineering acumen.

Although sales of Lamborghini tractors have been limited in the UK in recent years in favour of the Deutz-Fahr brand, quite a few are still at work on British farms, such as this Devon-based Racing 190.